God Made Outer Space

WRITTEN BY HENO HEAD, JR.

ILLUSTRATED BY RUSTY FLETCHER

Published by Standard Publishing, Cincinnati, Ohio
www.standardpub.com

ISBN-13: 978-0-7847-1702-8
ISBN-10: 0-7847-1702-8

16 15 14 13 12 11   8 9 10 11 12 13 14 15 16

Standard®
PUBLISHING

Cincinnati, Ohio

The Bible's first words are "In the beginning God created the heavens and earth." Before creation all was dark and empty, lonely and quiet.

Create means "to make." When God created, he made things. He made lots of things to fill the place we call OUTER SPACE. He scattered stars across space, sparkling up the darkness.

God didn't
make all stars
the same size.
That would
be too boring.
Instead, he
made some stars
HUGE.

Others are
MEDIUM SIZE.

And some
are SMALL.

In church or school, you may get stars for doing good work. Those stars usually look like this.

But God made his stars round.

The MILKY WAY is the name of our galaxy. The stars
we see at night are part of that galaxy. Milky Way stars
are sprinkled across our nighttime sky like sugar on
blackberries.

As we look at the stars at night, we can see patterns in
the sky. These patterns are called CONSTELLATIONS.

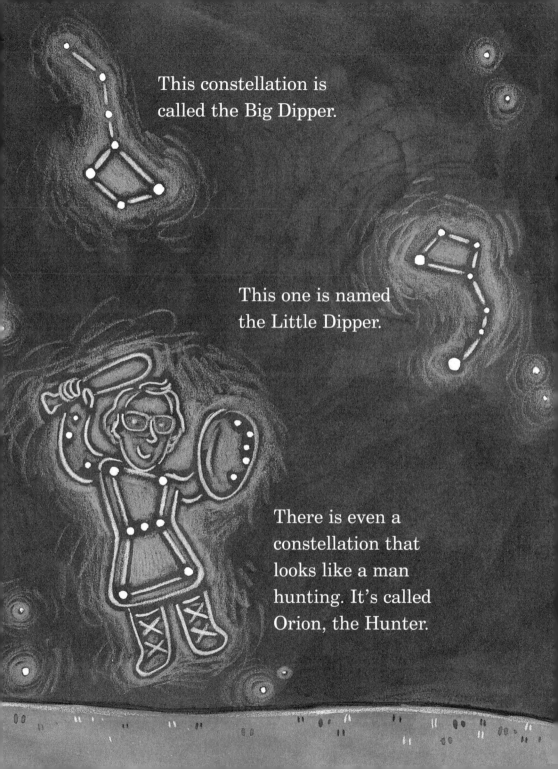

This constellation is called the Big Dipper.

This one is named the Little Dipper.

There is even a constellation that looks like a man hunting. It's called Orion, the Hunter.

Of all the stars God made, there is one we really like.
It's the closest to us, and it's called the SUN. Compared
to other stars, the Sun is just medium size. It's hot,
yellow, round, and bright.

The Sun is made of hot gases that produce lots of energy. We see the Sun's energy as sunlight, and we feel it as heat.

Earth seems like a pretty big place to us, but the Sun is much, much bigger than Earth. Over a hundred Earths could fit side by side across the middle of the Sun.

If the Sun were hollow, it would take a million Earths to fill it up.

God put the Earth at just the right distance from the Sun.

Not too close, or we would get too hot. *Whew!*

Not too far, or we would be too cold. *Brrrr!*

But just right.

Earth is called a PLANET. A planet is
a ball of rock or gas, or both, that travels
around a star. We are in a family with seven
other planets. The eight planets, plus the sun,
make up what we call the SOLAR SYSTEM.

In order from the sun, the
eight planets are:

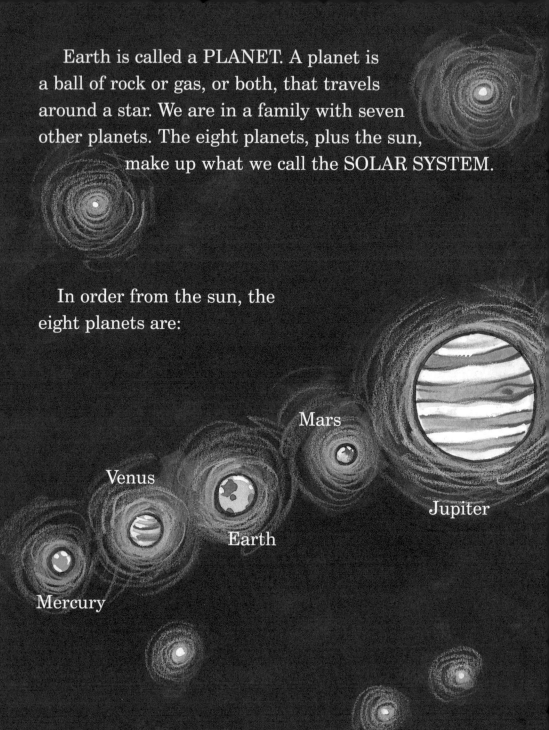

Mars

Venus

Jupiter

Earth

Mercury

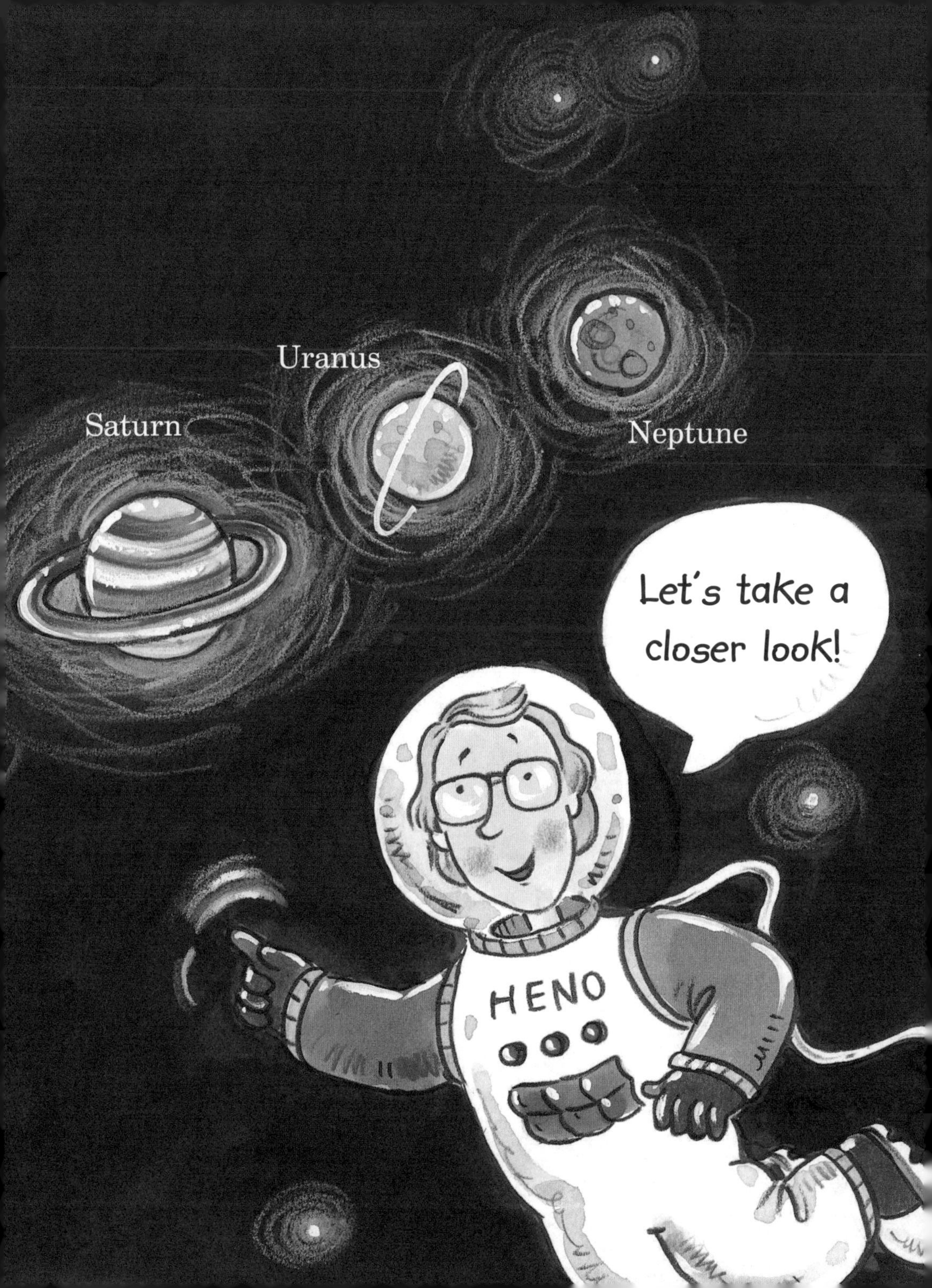
Uranus
Saturn
Neptune
Let's take a closer look!
HENO

Along with the planets, God made MOONS. Moons are smaller bodies that travel around planets. The moons shine by reflecting light from the Sun.

Earth has one moon. Mars has two moons. Saturn has 20 moons! Poor Mercury and Venus . . . they have no moons at all.

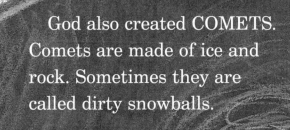

God also created COMETS.
Comets are made of ice and
rock. Sometimes they are
called dirty snowballs.

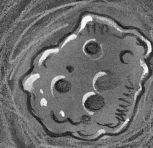

He made ASTEROIDS too.
Asteroids are large rocks found
between Mars and Jupiter.

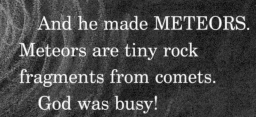

And he made METEORS.
Meteors are tiny rock
fragments from comets.
God was busy!